Published by Creative Education
P.O. Box 227, Mankato, Minnesota 56002
Creative Education is an imprint of The Creative Company
www.thecreativecompany.us

Design and Production by The Design Lab
Printed in the United States of America

Photographs by 123RF (Alex Lapuerta Mediavilla), Corbis (James L. Amos, Bettmann,
Images.com, Wolfgang Kaehler, Douglas Peebles, Kevin Schafer, Hubert Stadler, Stapleton
Collection, Stuart Westmorland), Getty Images (Walter Bibikow), iStockphoto (Matt Naylor)

Library of Congress Cataloging-in-Publication Data
Riggs, Kate.
Easter Island / by Kate Riggs.
p. cm. — (Places of old)
Includes index.
ISBN 978-1-58341-710-2
1. Prehistoric peoples—Easter Island—Juvenile literature.
2. Sculpture, prehistoric—Easter Island—Juvenile literature.
3. Polynesians—Easter Island—Antiquities—Juvenile literature.
4. Easter Island—Antiquities—Juvenile literature. I. Title. II. Series.
F3169.R54 2008   996.1'8—dc22   2007051901

First edition

2 4 6 8 9 7 5 3 1

EASTER ISLAND

by Kate Riggs

CREATIVE EDUCATION

EASTER ISLAND is a small piece of land in the middle of the Pacific Ocean. It is far away from any other island.

It is famous for its big statues. The statues are called *moai* (*MO-eye*).

Moai were all made out of large, single blocks of stone

Easter Island is an old place. The first people who lived there were called the Rapa Nui (*RAH-puh NOO-ee*). They were the ones who built the statues. They built almost 900 statues. They put the statues in different places around the island.

6

The people on Easter Island had to grow or raise all their own food. They could not get it from other places.

People can only imagine what the *moai* first looked like

To make the statues, the Rapa Nui used stone from a huge quarry. The stone was called tuff. It was softer than most rocks. That made it easier to carve.

8

Some of the moai *are so heavy and old that they are sinking into the ground.*

The Rapa Nui also made carvings out of wood

Some *moai* are just giant heads without bodies

Most *moai* do not face the ocean as this one does

Some of the *moai* are along the coast. They look like they are guarding the island. The statues may have helped the people worship their gods. But no one knows for sure why the statues were made.

The Rapa Nui may have held dances around the *moai*

The *moai* look like giant people. Their heads are very long. They have very large noses. The *moai* look like they are standing up, but they do not have any legs. Their arms hang straight at their sides.

Usually, several *moai* can be found grouped together

The hands of most *moai* have long, thin fingers

Most of the moai *sit in rows on big, flat stones called* ahu *(*AH-hoo*).*

14

Many *moai* lie in broken pieces on the ground

Sometimes, the Rapa Nui did not get along. They damaged each other's *moai*. By the 1900s, all of the *moai* had been knocked over.

There are hardly any trees on Easter Island today. The land is very rocky.

The Rapa Nui cut down many trees to make objects

People from other countries started coming to Easter Island in the 1900s. They found what was left of the *moai*. They started restoring the statues to look the way they used to.

About 24,000 people visit Easter Island each year. They get there on airplanes or boats.

People who restore the *moai* also measure them

The coast of Easter Island is rocky in many places

An explorer from the country of Holland named the island "Easter" after the holiday.

Now lots of visitors come to Easter Island. People like going there in December and January. It is summertime on the island then. People have to drink lots of water because it is hot and sunny most of the time.

People enjoy visiting the *moai* at any time of day

The story of the Easter Island statues
is still a mystery. But one thing people

People don't know why some *moai* are not on *ahu*

know is that there is nothing like them in the whole world!

About 900 *moai* have been found on Easter Island

glossary

coast
the edge of the land closest to the water

Pacific Ocean
the biggest ocean in the world; it is between the
United States and Asia

quarry
a big, deep hole in the ground where people dig
for stone

restoring
bringing something back to the way it used to be
or look

read more about it

Barron, T. A. *The Day the Stones Walked.* New York: Philomel/Penguin, 2007.

Pelta, Kathy. *Rediscovering Easter Island: How History Is Invented.* Minneapolis: Lerner Publishing Group, 2001.

index